How to Build a PYRAMID

When You Have No Idea What You're Doing

Abrar Nari

PORTRAIT
LIBRARY

Title: How to Build a Pyramid–When You Have No Idea What You're Doing

Author: Abrar Nari

First Edition: 2026

ISBN: 9788199784413

First published by: Portrait Library 2026

CONTENTS

Character Sketches iv

An Introduction viii

1. The Mastaba Monotony 1

2. A Promotion of Panic 13

3. The Grumpy Guardian of the Dunes 31

4. The Square Base & the Round Problem 45

5. The Quarry Quandary 59

6. The Ramp Riddle 69

7. The Alignment Fiasco 77

8. Mutiny on the Mid-Level 85

9. The Capstone Catastrophe 95

10. The Return of the Prodigy 105

11. Sand in the Royal Court 121

12. A Monument to Mayhem 129

CHARACTER SKETCHES

Reni (The Accidental Hero)

Role: Protagonist, Scribe-turned-Master-Builder.

Appearance: Scrawny, with ink-stained fingers and perpetually messy hair. Has expressive, wide eyes that convey either panic or wonder.

Personality: Anxious, earnest, and hopelessly optimistic. He is a terrible artist and a clumsy scribe, but he has a brilliant mind for logistics and people-management once he gains confidence. His growth from a nervous wreck to a confident leader is the heart of the story.

Fantasy Element: His connection to Khef; he becomes the "interpreter" of magic to men.

Khef, short for Khefre (The Divine Disaster)

Role: Mentor (of sorts), Magical Catalyst, Comic Relief.

Appearance: Not solid. He is a being of swirling, intelligent sand, who can condense into a vaguely human-like form or the shape of a desert animal (like a sarcastic fennec fox or a lazy scarab beetle). His "voice" is like the whispering of sand.

Personality: Sarcastic, ancient, and profoundly bored. He finds human ambition hilarious and our methods needlessly complicated. His help is always genius but delivered with a heavy side of mockery. Deep down, he's fond of Reni's determination and begins to enjoy the creative challenge.

Fantasy Element: A Sand Djinn/Spirit ("Shifter"). Can manipulate sand and stone on a large scale, create complex illusions, and possesses ancient, forgotten knowledge of physics and geology.

Pharaoh Djoser (The Divine Client)

Role: The Benefactor and Source of Ultimate Pressure.

Appearance: Impeccably dressed, with a false beard that is always slightly askew because he fidgets when excited. Has a habit of speaking in grand, dramatic pronouncements.

Personality: Not a tyrant, but a visionary with a very short attention span. He's less concerned with how it's done and more with when it will be done and how impressive it will look. His random visits to the site to suggest "just adding a giant sphinx on the side" are a recurring source of stress.

Fantasy Element: Believes he is a literal god, and the story never confirms or denies it, adding to the humor.

Imhotep (The Original Genius)

Role: Antagonist (indirectly), The Rival.

Appearance: Sharp, intense, always holding a measuring cord and a tablet of calculations. Looks like he hasn't slept in weeks.

Personality: A perfectionist and a purist. He believes in rigid geometry and proven methods. He sees Reni's (Khef's) chaotic, successful methods as heretical and an insult to the "pure art of architecture." His return creates the main conflict of the third act.

Bak (The Backbone of the Operation)

Role: Forewoman of the Labor Crews.

Appearance: Tall, muscular, and practical. Wears simple linen and a look of perpetual no-nonsense.

Personality: Tough, fair, and deeply respected by the workers. She is initially skeptical of the young, clueless Reni but grows to respect his (seemingly) bizarre but effective ideas and his genuine care for the workers' well-being. She is the "real" authority on the ground.

Medju (The Loyal Oaf)

Role: Reni's personally assigned (and slightly dim) royal guard.

Appearance: A mountain of a man who barely fits through doorways.

Personality: Incredibly loyal, incredibly strong, and not blessed with a surplus of brains. He takes his job of protecting Reni very seriously, often misinterpreting sneezes as assassination attempts. Provides excellent physical comedy.

The Workers (A Collective Character):

A diverse group of stone masons, haulers, carvers, and water-bearers. They are the chorus of confusion, amazement, and grumbling. They are the ones who have to implement Khef's wild plans, and their reactions (from thinking Reni is a madman to believing he's touched by the gods) provide a great barometer for the story's progress.

AN INTRODUCTION

Let us be perfectly, unequivocally clear about one thing: most of what you think you know about history is wrong.

This is not because historians are lazy or archaeologists are unobservant. It is because the truth is, and has always been, significantly stranger, more chaotic, and far more amusing than any of us are comfortable admitting. The grand, sweeping narratives of human achievement–the rise of civilizations, the construction of wonders, the very fabric of our past–often overlook a simple, fundamental truth: someone, somewhere, was having a truly disastrous day.

This book is the first in a series dedicated to correcting the record. It is an effort to peel back the varnish of time and reveal the splattered paint, the bent nails, and the panicked, improvisational genius that truly built our world. We are not dealing in dry facts and carbon-dated pottery shards. We are dealing in the currency of chaos: the desperate prayers of the unqualified, the grumpy interventions of ancient beings, and a startling number of happy accidents that were later, very seriously, labelled as 'divine inspiration'.

Take, for instance, the Great Pyramid of Giza. You have been taught it was a feat of unparalleled engineering, a testament to the power of a god-king and the mathematical precision of his priests. What you haven't been taught is that it was also a monument to creative desperation, a project saved from catastrophic failure by a well-meaning scribe, a disgruntled sand-spirit, and the strategic application of water to make things less screechy.

This is not a book of magic. It is a book of problems. And the solutions, while occasionally involving a being made of sentient sand, were almost always rooted in a simple, overlooked logic—the kind of logic that occurs to you when you are out of options, out of time, and staring into the abyss of a Pharaoh's disappointment.

So, if you are ready to trade dusty dogma for a dustier, but far more entertaining, reality, then read on. The following account is the true story of how a mountain was built, not through flawless divine decree, but through a series of brilliantly managed fiascos. It is, in short, the story of how things actually get done.

1. The Mastaba Monotony

The sun over Memphis had all the gentle warmth of a baker's oven at noon. It baked the mud-brick buildings, shimmered on the surface of the Nile, and made the air in the royal archives thick enough to taste. For Reni, junior scribe of the third grade, it was a perfectly ordinary, perfectly miserable afternoon.

He was supposed to be copying the grain yield reports from the Upper Kingdom. His reed brush hovered over a fresh sheet of papyrus, but his attention was elsewhere. On a large, discarded piece of limestone flake, he was attempting, for the third time, to sketch a design. It was supposed to be a structure, something grander than the boxy, flat-topped mastaba tombs that dotted the desert's edge. This one had sides that sloped, meeting at a point high in the sky. The result, unfortunately, looked less like a piercing monument to the gods and more like a drunken triangle trying to find its balance.

A drop of sweat fell from his brow, landing on the sketch and blurring the apex into an even more pathetic smudge.

"By the feathers of Ma'at," a voice hissed beside him.

"Are you crying on the records again, Reni?"

It was Hetepi, senior scribe. Hetepi had a face that seemed permanently pinched, as if he'd just smelled a fish three days past its prime. He was a man who found profound personal satisfaction in the correct alignment of a column of numbers.

"No, Hetepi. Just… condensation," Reni mumbled, quickly covering his failed sketch with the official grain report.

"Condensation is for the river, not for the archives. Your totals for the Abydos district are off by two hundred sacks. Again." Hetepi placed a perfectly manicured finger on Reni's papyrus. "Your 'four' looks suspiciously like a 'nine'. It's a fundamental failure of character."

Reni sighed. It was always a fundamental failure of something. His ink was too runny, his script too flamboyant, his postures during copying insufficiently rigid. He dreamed of concepts–grand designs, logistical marvels–while the world demanded precision.

"I'll redo it," Reni said, his shoulders slumping further.

"See that you do. The Pharaoh's prosperity depends on our accuracy. Not," Hetepi added, glancing at the limestone flake, "on your... artistic dabblings."

*****

In the royal courtyard, the air was marginally cooler, but the tension was far thicker. Pharaoh Djoser, Lord of the Two Lands, He of the Sedge and Bee, was frowning. Before him, standing next to a beautifully detailed clay model, was Imhotep, Chief Architect, High Priest of Ptah, and the wisest man in Egypt, who was currently feeling a profound and building pressure behind his eyes.

"It's... very square, Imhotep," Djoser said, prodding the model with a sceptre.

"It is a mastaba, Your Divine Majesty," Imhotep replied, his voice tight. "They are, by definition, square. Or rectangular. Geometrically stable."

"Stable." Djoser let the word hang in the air. He walked around the model, his brow furrowed. "Stable is good. Stable is what we want for our eternal rest. But is it… inspiring?" He gestured vaguely towards the sky. "When my *ka* ascends to join *Ra* in his solar barque, I want to look down and see a home that says, 'Behold, the dwelling of a god!' Not, 'Behold, a very stable, very square box.' My grandfather has a mastaba. My great-grandfather has a mastaba. I," he declared, thumping his chest, "am having a mastaba crisis."

Imhotep took a slow, measured breath. He had been designing and supervising the construction of the Pharaoh's eternal resting place for two years. He had planned the burial chambers, the ceremonial courtyards, the intricate tunnels to confuse tomb robbers. He was a man of structure, of mathematics, of divine proportions. He was not a man equipped for a royal crisis of architectural identity.

"Divine One, the mastaba is a proven form. It is timeless. It is—"

"It's boring," the Pharaoh interrupted, his divine lower lip protruding just a fraction. "I had a dream, Imhotep. A vision. A mountain of stone, its sides smooth and gleaming, pointing directly to the heavens. A stairway for a god. Can you make me a mountain?"

Imhotep stared. A mountain. He could calculate the load-bearing weight of limestone. He could align a corridor with the pole star. But a mountain? The sheer, audacious, logistical insanity of it made his eye twitch.

"A… mountain, Your Majesty? Of stone?"

"Yes! But a perfect, geometric mountain. Not a messy, natural one. A god's mountain." Djoser's eyes were alight with enthusiasm. "Can you do it?"

The pressure behind Imhotep's eyes intensified into a steady throb. "The workforce… the quarrying… the engineering… it is… unprecedented."

"Exactly!" Djoser beamed. "I don't want precedent. I want a pyramid."

The word hung in the air, strange and new. Pyramid.

"I... will need to consult the texts. To make new calculations," Imhotep said, his voice barely a whisper.

"Splendid!" The Pharaoh clapped his hands, dismissing him. "Start tomorrow. I want to see models. Exciting ones!"

*****

Back in the archives, Reni was on an errand, sent to fetch the tax records for the Delta region. This meant navigating the labyrinthine storage rooms, a place he loved. It was quiet, dusty, and filled with the ghosts of a thousand forgotten administrative projects. As he passed a niche filled with scrolls on seasonal flood patterns, he heard voices from the adjacent chamber—the office of the Royal Architects.

He recognized the tense, clipped tone of Imhotep. "...a mountain, Ankhmahor! A perfect, geometric mountain! The man wants to build a mountain in the desert!" A lower, calmer voice replied, belonging to Ankhmahor, Imhotep's chief draftsman. "The concept is… grand, Master. Perhaps we could begin with a larger mastaba? The largest ever built?"

"And put a smaller one on top of it?" Imhotep's voice was laced with a sarcasm so sharp it could cut granite. "No, no. He doesn't want a stack of boxes. He wants sides. Sloping sides. Do you have any idea what that does to the structural integrity? The weight distribution? It's an invitation to catastrophic collapse!"

Reni, frozen in place, felt a thrill run through him. A mountain. Sides that sloped. He peeked around the corner. Imhotep was pacing, his hands clutching his head. On a large table were clay models, not just of mastabas, but of structures with stepped sides, with slanted walls. One of them looked remarkably like the smudged sketch Reni had just made.

"The quarry masters say the new site at Tura has the finest white limestone," Ankhmahor offered, trying to be helpful.

"And how, pray tell, do we get a block of Tura

limestone, weighing as much as twenty men, onto a foundation that is a hundred cubits in the air?" Imhotep stopped his pacing and picked up a small, pyramid-like model. He stared at it, his face a mask of concentration and despair. "We would need ramps of such a size they would require their own workforce. The volume of material for the ramps would exceed the volume of the tomb itself! It's mathematically obscene!"

He held the model aloft, his hand trembling slightly from fatigue and frustration. "It is an elegant shape. I grant you that. A beautiful, simple, impossible shape."

And then, it happened.

Whether it was the sweat on his palm from his frantic pacing, or a tiny, unseen flaw in the clay, or simply the universe deciding it was time for a change, the model slipped.

It seemed to fall in slow motion, tumbling end over end. Imhotep and Ankhmahor watched, horrified, as it descended towards the hard-packed earthen floor.

Crunch.

The sound was small, final, and deeply symbolic. The perfect, geometric mountain was now a pile of shards.

There was a long, profound silence. Imhotep stared at the fragments. He did not shout. He did not curse. He simply went very, very still.

"Master?" Ankhmahor ventured, his voice timid.

Imhotep slowly straightened his back. He looked at the dust on his fingers, then at the broken pieces of his ambition, and finally at the wide-eyed, terrified face of Reni, who had just witnessed the entire event.

"Tell the Pharaoh," Imhotep said, his voice eerily calm, "that his Chief Architect is going for a walk."

"A… a walk, Master? For how long?"

"Indefinitely," Imhotep said. He carefully removed his official seal of office, the mark of the Chief Builder, and placed it gently on the table amidst the clay rubble. "I feel a sudden, overwhelming need to… find myself. I believe I may have misplaced my sanity somewhere near the Tura quarry. It should be easy to spot; it will be the one laughing hysterically."

And with that, the wisest man in Egypt, the High Priest of Ptah, turned on his heel and walked out of his office, out of the palace, and into the shimmering heat of the afternoon, leaving a stunned draftsman and a petrified junior scribe in his wake.

Reni looked from the empty doorway to the seal of the Chief Builder, gleaming innocently on the table. It was the most powerful administrative object in the kingdom, short of the Pharaoh's own crook and flail. And it was just… sitting there. A cold dread, entirely separate from the desert heat, began to pool in his stomach. He had a terrible, sinking feeling that his days of quietly messing up grain reports were about to come to a very abrupt and very, very loud end.

2. A Promotion of Panic

The silence Imhotep left behind was a physical presence, thick and heavy as a funeral shroud. It was broken by a small, dry cough from Ankhmahor. The draftsman's eyes were wide, darting from the shattered clay on the floor to the vacant doorway, then to the official seal on the table, as if it were a scorpion poised to strike.

Reni, realizing he had been holding his breath, let it out in a slow, shaky stream. He took a hesitant step into the room. "Master Ankhmahor? Is… is he coming back?"

Ankhmahor didn't seem to hear him. He reached out a trembling finger and poked the seal, as if to confirm its reality. "He's gone to find his sanity," he muttered to himself. "By Ptah's strong hands, he's actually done it." He looked at Reni, his expression one of pure, unadulterated catastrophe. "You. Scribe. Did you witness this?"

Reni nodded mutely, his throat tight.

"Then you are a witness to the end of all our careers," Ankhmahor declared with grim finality. He began to pace, mimicking his former master's path. "The Pharaoh wants a mountain. Imhotep has resigned. The project is in ruins. We are all going to be measuring sand in the Western Desert for the rest of our short, miserable lives."

The cold dread in Reni's stomach solidified into a block of ice. Measuring sand was the euphemism for the most tedious, dead-end job in the kingdom, reserved for those who had displeased the crown. He saw his future unfold before him: a tiny, dusty hut, an endless expanse of dunes, and a broken abacus.

"Perhaps… perhaps he'll calm down?" Reni offered, his voice squeaking slightly. "The heat… it can affect the mind…"

"Imhotep's mind is a tempered bronze instrument. If it has broken, it is broken for good." Ankhmahor stopped pacing and fixed Reni with a desperate stare. "You. You must go to the Vizier. You are a neutral party. A scribe. You report what you have seen. Tell him… tell him the Chief Architect has taken a sudden leave of absence for health reasons."

"Me?" Reni's voice cracked. "But I'm just… I'm fetching tax records."

"You are now the bearer of catastrophic news," Ankhmahor said, seizing Reni's arm and propelling him towards the door. "It is a sacred, if undesirable, duty. Go! Now! Before the Pharaoh asks for an update on his mountain!"

*****

The office of the Vizier, Merptah, was a study in organized power. The walls were lined with papyrus scrolls, each a thread in the vast tapestry of the kingdom's administration. Merptah himself was a man who resembled a benevolent, well-fed hippopotamus. He was calm, methodical, and believed that every problem, from a Nile flood to a royal tantrum, could be solved with the correct application of paperwork.

He looked up as Reni was ushered in by a guard, his brow furrowing slightly at the sight of the young, ink-stained, and visibly terrified scribe.

"Yes? I am rather busy reconciling the quarterly offerings to the temple of Hathor. This had better be urgent."

Reni swallowed, his mouth dry as desert sand. "V-Vizier Merptah. I bring news from the Office of the Royal Architect."

Merptah put down his brush. "Imhotep has new calculations? Excellent. The Pharaoh has asked three times this morning."

"Not… not exactly, your Eminence." Reni took a deep breath, trying to channel Hetepi's monotone delivery. "Chief Architect Imhotep has… relinquished his post. He has departed the palace. He stated an intention to… find his sanity."

The Vizier's placid expression did not change. He blinked slowly. "Relinquished his post," he repeated, his tone flat.

"Yes, your Eminence."

"He has gone to find his sanity."

"That is what he said, your Eminence."

"And he left his seal?"

Reni nodded, the movement jerky. "On the table. Amidst… the rubble of a model."

Merptah leaned back in his chair, steepling his fingers. The only sound in the room was the faint buzz of a fly trapped near the ceiling. Reni waited for the explosion, for the roar of fury, for the call to the guards to seize the messenger of bad news.

Instead, Merptah sighed, a long, weary sound. "The project has been a strain," he said, almost to himself. "The Pharaoh's… enthusiasm… is not always matched by a grasp of practicalities." He looked at Reni. "You are the scribe who witnessed this? Reni, isn't it? You work in the central archives."

Reni was stunned that the Vizier knew his name. "Y-yes, your Eminence."

"And you are certain of what you saw? He did not merely step out for a breath of air?"

"He said 'indefinitely,' your Eminence. He was very… calm."

"A bad sign," Merptah murmured. "Very well. You have performed your duty. Return to your post."

A wave of relief so powerful it made him dizzy washed over Reni. He had delivered the news and survived. He bowed deeply and practically fled from the room.

Merptah, left alone, picked up a fresh sheet of papyrus. He dipped his brush in ink and began to write in a neat, unhurried script. 'Memorandum: Regarding the Vacancy of the Post of Chief Architect…' He worked for a few minutes, then sanded the ink and rolled the scroll. He summoned a messenger.

"See that this reaches the Pharaoh's private secretary immediately."

*****

Reni's relief was short-lived. He had barely returned to his stool in the archives, his heart rate just beginning to settle, when Hetepi appeared, his pinched face looking almost… impressed.

"Reni. The Vizier's office summons you. Immediately."

The ice block was back. "Again? But I just—"

"Do not question, do not delay," Hetepi snapped, though there was a curious glint in his eye. "It seems your… unique talents… have been noted at the highest level."

This could not be good. Reni's mind raced as he was led back to the Vizier's chamber. Had he misspoken? Had Imhotep returned and denied everything? Was he to be made the scapegoat?

When he entered, the room was different. The Vizier was not alone. Pharaoh Djoser himself was there, pacing with an energy that was the polar opposite of Imhotep's despairing stalk. He looked… excited.

"Ah! The witness!" Djoser boomed, pointing his sceptre at Reni. "The one who saw the great artist's spirit take flight!"

Reni dropped to his knees, pressing his forehead to the cool stone floor. "Your Divine Majesty."

"Rise, rise! Let me look at you." Djoser circled Reni

as if he were a new breed of goat. "Young. Good. The old ways have failed. We need new blood. Fresh ideas!"

Reni risked a glance at Merptah, who gave a slight, almost imperceptible shrug.

"Your Majesty," the Vizier interjected smoothly. "While young Reni here is a diligent scribe, the post of Chief Architect traditionally requires decades of experience in—"

"Experience!" Djoser waved a dismissive hand. "Experience gave us mastabas! I am done with experience. I want inspiration. This one," he said, clapping a heavy, bejewelled hand on Reni's shoulder, making his knees buckle, "was there at the moment of creative rupture! He saw the old model break! He understands what we are moving from. That is half the battle!"

"But, Your Majesty, the practicalities…" Merptah tried again.

"Are details!" the Pharaoh declared. "This is a sign from the gods. Imhotep's spirit ascends, and a new one is placed in our path." He turned his radiant, slightly unhinged gaze upon Reni. "Scribe Reni. I am appointing you Acting Chief Architect of the Royal Necropolis Project. You will build me my mountain."

The world swam before Reni's eyes. The walls seemed to tilt. He heard a distant roaring in his ears. "I… Your Majesty… I copy grain reports."

"And now you will copy the heavens onto the earth!" Djoser beamed. "Merptah, see that he has everything he needs. Full authority. I want to see a new model in three days." And with that, the Lord of the Two Lands swept out of the room, leaving behind the scent of myrrh and impending doom.

The silence returned. Reni stood, swaying slightly. He looked at the Vizier, his eyes pleading.

Merptah studied him for a long moment. He saw a young man on the precipice of a catastrophic failure that would likely get him buried in a very small, very un-pyramid-like hole. He felt a flicker of pity.

"It would seem," Merptah said, his voice dry, "that you have been promoted."

"I can't… I don't know how to build a pyramid," Reni whispered, the truth of it crushing him.

"No one does," Merptah replied calmly. "That is the essence of the problem. But the Pharaoh has spoken. You are now in charge of solving the unsolvable." He picked up Imhotep's seal, which a servant had brought from the architect's office. It felt impossibly heavy in his hand. He held it out to Reni.

Reni stared at it. The carved stone symbol of an office he was uniquely unqualified to hold. Taking it felt like accepting a death sentence.

"What… what is the first thing I should do?" Reni asked, his voice hollow.

Merptah considered the question. "The first thing? I would suggest," he said, with the ghost of a sympathetic smile, "that you go and look at the site. And then, perhaps, pray. A great deal."

*****

The Royal Necropolis site was a buzzing, chaotic expanse of ordered activity that was, to Reni's eyes, completely incomprehensible. Thousands of workers moved with purpose. Teams of laborers hauled sledges loaded with stone blocks. Masons chiselled with rhythmic taps. Foremen bellowed instructions. It was a machine, a vast, living machine, and he had just been placed at its controls with no idea what any of the levers did.

He stood at the edge of the cleared desert plateau, the Vizier's two stern guards flanking him, a silent reminder of his new, unwanted status. The foundation of the grand mastaba was already laid out, a perfect, enormous square of limestone that now seemed pathetically inadequate. The scale of it all was overwhelming. The dust, the noise, the sheer mass of the enterprise—it stole the breath from his lungs.

A woman with a no-nonsense posture and arms corded with muscle approached him. She held a wax tablet covered in tallies. She looked him up and down, her eyes lingering on his clean linen kilt and soft scribe's hands.

"You're the new one?" she asked, her voice raspy from dust and command. "I am Bak, foreman of the hauling crews. We heard Imhotep lost his mind. They didn't say they were replacing him with a boy."

Reni flinched. "I am Reni. The Pharaoh has… placed me in charge." Bak's expression did not change. "Fine. We're short on copper for the cutting saws. The ramp for the foundation stones is collapsing under its own weight. The water carriers are complaining their rations have been cut. What are your orders, Chief Architect?"

The words hit him like physical blows. Copper? Ramps? Water rations? These were problems for… for someone else. For Imhotep. He had no answers. He had only a terrifying, yawning emptiness where his confidence should be.

"I… I will need to… assess the situation," he stammered.

Bak's lips tightened into a thin line. "Assess quickly. The men don't like uncertainty. It makes them wonder if they'll get paid." She turned and walked away, her disdain a palpable force.

Reni stood there, the impostor, the boy-architect. The workers glanced at him as they passed, their looks a mixture of curiosity and contempt. The sun beat down, and the weight of the seal in his belt felt like it was dragging him through the earth. Merptah's advice echoed in his mind.

Pray. A great deal.

He had to get away. He couldn't think here, surrounded by the evidence of his own incompetence.

"I am going to… to seek divine inspiration," he announced to the guards, his voice trembling only slightly. "I will be in the high desert. Do not follow me."

He didn't wait for a response. He turned and walked away from the site, away from the noise and the expectations, towards the silent, rolling dunes that bordered the plateau. It wasn't a plan. It was an escape. But as he trudged up the first sandy slope, the frantic pounding of his heart began to slow. The silence out here was vast, broken only by the whisper of the wind.

He climbed until the construction site was a mere anthill in the distance, until he was alone in a world of sand and sky. He sank to his knees, the fine grains warm between his fingers.

"Okay," he whispered to the empty horizon. "Okay. I am here. I'm… assessing." He looked up at the endless blue. "If anyone is listening… I am in desperate, desperate need of a sign. A small one would suffice. A hint. A… a slightly less impossible idea."

The wind sighed around him, offering nothing but more sand.

He sighed, a sound of utter defeat. "Or just strike me down now. That would also solve the problem."

He waited. The sun continued to shine. The dunes remained impassive.

Feeling foolish, and more alone than he had ever felt in his life, Reni bowed his head. It was then, in the profound quiet, that he noticed something strange. The sand directly in front of him was shifting. Not from the wind, which was blowing steadily from the north. This sand was moving against the breeze, swirling gently, gathering itself as if with purpose.

He blinked, thinking it a trick of the light, a result of his panic and the desert heat. But the movement continued. The grains danced and coalesced, rising in a small, lazy vortex. They began to form a shape. A simple, elegant, three-dimensional shape.

A perfect, miniature pyramid.

It stood about a hand's breadth high, its edges sharp, its sides smooth. It was a flawless, geometric mountain of sand.

Reni stared, his mind refusing to process what his eyes were seeing. He reached out a tentative finger, half-expecting the shape to collapse.

Before he could touch it, the sand pyramid dissolved with a soft hiss, falling back into the dune. The sand settled. And then, a new sound reached him, not the wind, but a voice—dry, ancient, and laced with profound irritation.

"A 'slightly less impossible idea'?" the voice whispered from the very air around him. "You ask for so little. It's almost insulting."

3. The Grumpy Guardian of the Dunes

The voice was like the sound of a thousand ancient papyri rustling at once, dry and full of cracks, yet somehow clear and distinct in the vast silence. It seemed to come from everywhere and nowhere, from the sand beneath his knees and the air in his lungs.

Reni froze, his finger still outstretched towards the spot where the sand pyramid had been. His first, perfectly rational thought was that the sun had finally baked his brain. His second thought was that he was having a stroke, perhaps brought on by the sheer, overwhelming terror of his promotion. His third thought, which arrived with the force of a dropped stone, was that this might actually be the divine sign he'd asked for.

He slowly lowered his hand. "Hello?" he whispered, his voice cracking.

The only answer was a long, drawn-out sigh that seemed to emanate from the dune itself. "Hello," the voice repeated, the word dripping with weary sarcasm. "Is that the best you can manage? 'Hello?' I manifest a perfect, transient geo-architectural marvel from base matter, and your response is a social nicety."

Reni's mouth opened and closed. He looked around wildly, but there was nothing but rolling dunes and the immense, empty sky. "Who… what are you? Where are you?"

"I am here," the voice stated, as if it were the most obvious thing in the world. "And as for 'what'… I am the entity you so rudely awakened from a perfectly satisfactory ten-millennium nap. The vibrations. The frantic, panicked little prayers. It's like being tapped on the shoulder by a gnat. Repeatedly."

The sand in front of Reni began to shift again. This time, it didn't form a shape so much as it gathered itself into a concentrated, swirling column, about the height of a man. It was like a miniature, lazy tornado, but one that seemed to possess a keen and irritated intelligence. Within the swirling grains, two darker patches coalesced, focusing on him with unnerving intensity.

"You're… sand," Reni said, the observation feeling utterly inadequate.

The column seemed to bristle. "I inhabit the sand. I

am a Shifter. A spirit of the deep earth, the enduring stone, the patient dune. My name is Khef. And you are a very loud, very distressed mortal who has interrupted my slumber."

A spirit. A real, live—or at least, real—spirit. Reni's scribe-brain, trained for record-keeping, latched onto the name. "Khef. Short for Khefre?"

The sand column shuddered. "Do not utter that name. It's so… formal. It was given to me by a priest with a terribly pompous beard. Khef is fine. Now, state your business so I can dismiss it and return to my rest. You wanted a 'sign'. You have had one. A rather elegant one, if I may say so. Now, off you go."

The column began to sink, the sand grains starting to settle.

"Wait!" Reni cried, lurching forward. "You can't go!"

The sinking stopped. The two dark patches fixed on him again. "I can. I am. Watch me."

"No, I mean… I need more than a sign. I need… help." The word felt pathetic, but it was the truest thing he'd said all day.

Khef let out a sound that was somewhere between a groan and the hiss of shifting dunes. "Of course you do. You all do. 'Move this rock, Khef.' 'Find this lost trinket, Khef.' 'My camel has a limp, Khef.' It's always something. What is it this time? A lost child? A buried trinket? Speak quickly."

Reni took a deep breath, trying to order his thoughts. This was it. His only chance. "The Pharaoh… he wants me to build him a… a mountain. A pyramid."

There was a long, profound silence. The swirling sand slowed almost to a stop.

"A pyramid," Khef repeated, his tone flat.

"Yes. A huge one. Out of stone. Pointing to the sky."

The sand column contorted, as if the entity within was having a minor seizure. A sound emerged, a dry, rasping, choking noise that it took Reni a moment to recognize as laughter. It was not a joyful sound. It was the sound of cosmic, millennia-old disbelief.

"A pyramid?" Khef finally managed, his voice shaking with mirthless glee. "You? You can barely keep your knees from knocking together. You want to build a pyramid?"

"I don't want to!" Reni's frustration finally broke through his awe. "I have to! The Pharaoh commanded it! If I fail, they'll… I don't know what they'll do, but it will involve a lot of sand and no papyrus!"

"Ah," Khef said, the laughter ceasing abruptly. "A command performance. How droll. And so, you come to me. You wish for me to build your pyramid for you."

The hope that had begun to flutter in Reni's chest was immediately crushed by the sheer disdain in the spirit's voice. "No! Well… not… not for me. With me. I need… guidance."

"Guidance," Khef mused, the column swirling thoughtfully. "You need guidance on how to pile rocks on top of other rocks in a structurally sound and aesthetically pleasing manner. A problem that has, I note, been solved by termites for epochs. You are less inventive than an insect."

Reni felt his face grow hot. "Termites don't use stones

that weigh more than a family of hippos! They don't have to worry about ramps collapsing or workforces mutinying!"

"Details," Khef sniffed. "The principle is the same. Stable base, tapering sides. Even your own kind managed it with those ziggurat things up in Mesopotamia. Clumsy things, but the general idea was there."

"So you can help?" Reni pressed, seizing on the comment.

"I did not say that," Khef replied, his tone turning sharp. "I am a Shifter. I am of the deep, silent places. I am not a… a construction foreman. The constant noise, the pounding, the sheer, chaotic mess of a building site… it's anathema to me. It would be like asking a fish to supervise a forest fire."

"But you're awake now," Reni argued, a desperate cunning seeping into his voice. "And if I fail, I'll probably be sent out here, to the desert, to… to measure sand! I'll be here every day, miserable and loud, praying and complaining. My vibrations will be a constant nuisance. Wouldn't it be easier to just help me succeed, so I can go away and you can get back to your nap in peace?"

The sand column went perfectly still. The two dark patches seemed to be staring into his very soul. Reni held his breath. He had overplayed his hand. He was sure of it.

"You are more clever than you look," Khef said, his voice a low rumble. "A low bar, to be sure, but you have cleared it." He sighed, a sound of ultimate resignation. "There are… rules. Ancient pacts. If a mortal awakens us with a sincere plea, and binds us with a compelling argument, we are… obliged. To a point."

"Obliged?" Reni's heart began to beat faster.

"Do not get excited. It is a curse, not a blessing. For both of us." The column of sand began to condense, the grains packing tightly together, losing their swirling nature. They formed a solid, sculpted figure about three feet tall. It was a vaguely humanoid shape made entirely of packed, dark sand, with stumpy legs, a rounded body, and a featureless head save for the two deep, dark holes where its eyes should be. It looked like a grumpy, minimalist statue a child might make at the riverbank.

"This is less taxing," the now-solid Khef stated, his voice emanating from the featureless head. He took a stiff, crunching step forward. "Now. This 'obligation'. It is a binding. I will provide… consultation. I will offer solutions to the problems your species' delightful lack of foresight creates. But you will be the instrument. You will direct the workers. You will take the credit, or more likely, the blame. I will not move a single stone with my own power unless absolutely necessary. The effort is… vulgar."

Reni stared at the walking sand-figure. It was the most absurd, terrifying, and wonderful thing he had ever seen. "Consultation. So… you'll tell me what to do?"

"I will tell you how to solve the problems you encounter. You will have to translate my genius into terms your fellow mortals can understand. This will, I suspect, be the most challenging part of the entire endeavor." Khef took another step, his sandy feet making a soft shush-shush sound. "Do we have an accord?"

Reni didn't hesitate. What choice did he have? It was either a magical, grumpy sand-spirit or a lifetime of measuring sand. "Yes. We have an accord."

A faint, golden shimmer passed through Khef's sandy form, like a pulse of heat lightning. "It is done. The binding is sealed. Now, take me to this… project of yours. Let us survey the extent of the impending disaster." The sand-figure gestured a stumpy arm towards the distant plateau. "And do try to look like you're in charge. It will make this whole charade slightly less humiliating."

Reni stood up, his legs shaky. He began to walk back towards the site, the small, grumpy figure of Khef trudging alongside him, leaving a trail of tiny, perfect footprints in the sand.

As they neared the edge of the plateau and the noise of the site grew louder, Khef stopped. The din of thousands of workers, the shouts, the grinding of stone on stone, was a palpable wave.

"By the deep, silent earth," Khef muttered, his sandy form seeming to flinch. "It's even worse than I imagined. The noise. The disorganization." His dark eye-holes scanned the scene, taking in the half-built ramps, the piles of stone, the chaotic movement of men and animals. "They're just… pushing things. How primitive."

"It's how it's always been done," Reni said defensively.

"And look where it's gotten you," Khef retorted. "Stuck with a square foundation and a round problem." He pointed a sandy nub towards the main construction ramp, which was indeed showing signs of stress, its sides bulging. "See? They're fighting the sand. They treat it as an enemy. It's pathetic."

"What should we do?" Reni asked, feeling a flicker of hope. The spirit had identified a problem immediately.

"We?" Khef turned his blank face towards Reni. "You are going to go down there and act like you know what you're doing. I will observe from here. I need to understand the full, tragic scope of the situation. When you have a moment away from prying eyes, we will discuss the first lesson: the principle of fluid dynamics as applied to granular materials."

"The… what?"

Khef let out another dry, rattling sigh. "How to make the sand work for you, you imbecile. Now go. And for my sake, try to stand up straight. You're slouching like a condemned man."

Reni took a deep breath, squared his shoulders as best he could, and began the long walk down into the chaos. He could feel the eyes of the workers on him again. But this time, it was different. This time, he wasn't entirely alone. He had a consultant. A consultant made of sand who found his entire species ridiculous, but a consultant nonetheless.

He saw Bak watching him, her arms crossed. He met her gaze and gave a small, tight nod, which he hoped conveyed authority and not indigestion.

As he approached, she gestured with her chin towards the troubled ramp. "The ramp is failing. Do you have orders, Acting Chief Architect?"

Reni's mind went blank for a second, then he remembered Khef's words. They're fighting the sand.

He looked at the ramp, then at the workers straining to haul a sledge up its slope. He didn't know the principle of fluid dynamics, but he understood the concept of an enemy becoming an ally.

"Yes," he said, his voice stronger than he expected. "Stop the work on the ramp for today."

Bak's eyebrows shot up. "Stop? We are behind schedule as it is."

"The schedule is based on a flawed method," Reni said, parroting what he imagined Khef would say. "We are fighting the desert. From now on, we will work with it. Have the men bring water from the Nile. As much as they can."

Bak stared at him as if he had just suggested they build the pyramid out of cheese. "Water? For what?"

Reni allowed himself a small, mysterious smile, one that he hoped hid the fact that he had no earthly idea what he was talking about. "For the sand," he said. "We're going to teach it a new trick."

4. The Square Base & the Round Problem

The silence that followed Reni's pronouncement was broken only by the distant, rhythmic tap of a mason's chisel. Bak's face was a masterpiece of incredulity. Her arms, already crossed, tightened their grip as if physically restraining herself from shaking some sense into him.

"Water," she repeated, the word flat and heavy as a mud brick. "You want to pour the Nile onto the desert."

"Not the whole Nile," Reni clarified, his newfound confidence already beginning to waver under her stony gaze. "Just… a significant amount of it. For the sand on the ramp. To… firm it up."

He was winging it, stitching together Khef's cryptic comment about "working with the sand" and a half-remembered observation from his childhood, watching mud-brick makers slapping wet clay into molds. The logic felt flimsy, a spiderweb of hope and desperation.

Bak looked from his earnest, slightly sweaty face to the vast, sun-baked construction site, then back to him. She let out a short, sharp breath that was not quite a laugh. "The men will think you've lost your mind. They're haulers and stone-setters, not water-bearers for a child's mud-pie game."

"The men," Reni said, forcing a steadiness into his voice he did not feel, "are following the orders of the Chief Architect, as appointed by Pharaoh Djoser himself. If they have a problem with the method, they are welcome to take it up with his Divine Majesty." He paused, then added, "I'm sure he would be fascinated to hear their views on his mountain."

It was a low blow, invoking the Pharaoh's name as a shield, but Reni was learning fast. The politics of survival were as important as the physics of construction.

Bak's jaw tightened. She recognized the threat, veiled though it was. She gave a curt, jerky nod. "As you command." She turned and bellowed across the plateau, her voice cutting through the work-noise like a copper blade. "Hauling crews! Down tools! You're on water duty! Every pot, every skin, to the river and back! Move!"

A wave of confusion, then grumbling, rippled through the workforce. Men who had been heaving on ropes for hours looked at each other in bewilderment. Hauling water was women's work, children's work. It was a demotion. A series of disgruntled mutters rose into the air, aimed in Reni's general direction.

He stood his ground, trying to project an aura of serene, knowing authority, which was difficult when all he wanted to do was run back up the dune and ask Khef what in the name of *Ra* he was supposed to do next.

From his vantage point, Khef watched the proceedings with a sort of detached, academic interest. The little sand-figure had seated itself on a rocky outcrop, its stumpy legs dangling. It was, Reni thought, an oddly human posture for a being of ancient, elemental power.

"They're confused," Reni said, arriving at the outcrop, his shoulders slumping the moment he was out of sight of the workers. "They think it's a punishment. Or a joke."

"All progress looks like madness to those entrenched in failure," Khef stated, not turning his featureless head. "Observe."

He pointed a sandy nub. The first of the water-bearers was arriving, a bulky man named Medju—the same one who had been assigned as Reni's guard—who was carrying two large, sloshing pots with an expression of profound confusion. Bak directed him to pour the water at the base of the troubled ramp.

The water hit the hot, dry sand and vanished, leaving only a dark, damp stain that began to steam immediately.

"See?" Reni whispered, panic rising. "It's just soaking in! It's doing nothing!"

"Patience," Khef chided. "You cannot fill a cup with a single drop. Wait for the chorus."

More water-bearers arrived, a slow-moving line of them, and under Bak's impatient direction, they began dousing the lower section of the ramp. The initial stains spread, connecting, turning the light yellow sand to a dark, wet brown. The workers, now idle, gathered to watch, their arms crossed, their skepticism a tangible cloud.

Then, something changed. The fifth or sixth wave of water didn't just disappear. It pooled slightly. The sand, now saturated, began to hold its shape. A young worker, tasked with patting down a bulging section of the ramp with a tamper, brought his tool down. Instead of sinking in and sending a shower of dry grains flying, it landed with a firm, satisfying thud. The wet sand compacted, holding the impression of the tamper.

A murmur, different from the earlier grumbling, went through the crowd.

Bak, her own skepticism warring with the evidence before her, knelt and pressed her hand into the wet sand. It was firm, cohesive. She stood up, wiping her hand on her kilt, and looked at Reni, who had cautiously approached from the dunes. Her expression was no longer one of pure contempt. It was calculating.

"The sledges," she called out, her voice cutting through the murmurs. "Bring a test sledge."

A small, unladen wooden sledge was dragged forward and placed on the newly dampened ramp. Two men took the ropes. They braced themselves, expecting the usual back-breaking strain.

They pulled. The sledge slid forward with an unnerving, almost effortless ease. It didn't dig in. It didn't drag. It glided on the damp surface as if on a sheet of ice.

The silence this time was absolute. Every worker, every foreman, stared at the sliding sledge as if it were a miracle.

Reni's heart hammered against his ribs. It worked. It actually worked.

"The water," a worker whispered, his voice full of awe. "It makes the sand slippery."

"It's a blessing from Hapi!" another cried out, referring to the god of the Nile.

Reni saw his chance. He couldn't explain the science—Khef's "principle of fluid dynamics"—but he could channel the divine. He stepped forward, raising his hands.

"The Nile gives life to our fields," he announced, his voice ringing in the sudden quiet. "And now, Hapi grants his blessing to our work! We are not fighting the desert! We are using its own nature, with the gift of the river, to serve the Pharaoh's vision! This is not a punishment. This is a new way!"

He looked at Bak. "Soak the entire ramp. From now on, water the sand ahead of the sledges. Let the river do the work."

There was no grumbling now. The men looked at the effortlessly sliding sledge, then at the water pots, then at Reni with something entirely new: a flicker of respect. They moved with a new energy, not the sluggishness of forced labor, but the briskness of men who had witnessed a small, practical miracle.

Bak walked over to him. She didn't smile—Reni suspected she considered smiling a sign of weakness—but the permanent crease of frustration between her brows had softened slightly.

"It seems the sand has learned its trick," she said, her tone neutral. "The ramp will hold. For now."

It was the closest he would get to a compliment. He nodded, trying to look like he'd known it would work all along.

As the afternoon wore on, the efficiency of the work transformed. The endless, grinding struggle to haul stones up the ramp became a smoother, faster process. The mood on the plateau lightened. The workers, who had been on the verge of mutiny, were now animated, experimenting with the exact amount of water needed, calling out to each other with a newfound camaraderie.

Later, as the sun began to dip below the western cliffs, painting the sky in shades of orange and purple, Reni found a moment of solitude near the foundation stones. The day had been a victory, a narrow, desperate, but undeniable victory.

"So," he said quietly, to the empty air beside him. "Fluid dynamics."

A small pile of sand on a foundation stone stirred, and Khef's compact form reassembled itself. "Granular shear reduction facilitated by interstitial liquid bridging," the spirit stated, his tone that of a long-suffering tutor. "But 'slippery sand' is an acceptable, if intellectually barren, summary for your purposes."

"It worked," Reni said, a grin finally breaking through his carefully constructed mask of authority. "They think I'm a genius. Or a prophet."

"They are easily impressed," Khef replied drily. "You dampened some dirt. Do not let it go to your head. The ramp was the simplest of your problems. The foundation is next."

Reni looked down at the massive limestone blocks that formed the perfectly square base of what was to be the pyramid. "What's wrong with the foundation? Imhotep laid it out. It's perfectly square."

"Is it?" Khef asked. The sand-figure hopped down from the stone and walked to the southeastern corner of the foundation. "Your 'perfect' square is laid out on ground that is not perfectly level. The human eye is a crude instrument. By the time you build up a few courses, that tiny discrepancy will become a noticeable lean. Your mountain will list like a drunken boat on the Nile."

Reni's grin vanished. He peered at the foundation. It looked level. It looked square. But the absolute certainty in Khef's voice was unnerving. "How can you tell?"

"I can feel the pull of the earth," Khef said, as if explaining that water was wet. "The stone here is slightly lower than the stone there." He pointed from one corner to the opposite one. "It is the difference of a finger's width, but it is enough."

"So what do we do?" Reni asked, the familiar panic beginning to creep back. "We can't lift these stones to level the ground beneath them!"

"Of course not. That would be brutish. Inefficient." Khef's dark eye-holes seemed to gleam. "We will use the two things you have in abundance: water, and the desert's own patience. Tomorrow, you will instruct them to build a low, temporary wall of mud around the entire foundation, turning it into a giant, shallow basin."

"A basin?"

"Then, you will have them fill it with water from the

Nile. Let it sit for a day. The water, left to its own devices, will find its own level. It does not care for your crude measurements. It knows only the truth of the earth's pull."

Reni's mind, his scribe's mind, began to see it. A giant, flat sheet of water, defining a perfectly level plane. "Then… we mark the waterline on the foundation stones…"

"And you cut the subsequent courses of stone to that line," Khef finished. "A perfectly level base, achieved not by straining muscles, but by using the immutable laws of nature. It's almost elegant. For a mortal endeavor."

Reni looked out at the darkening site, at the workers heading back to their encampment, their voices tired but no longer resentful. He had solved one problem with water. Now, he would solve another. He wasn't just piling rocks. He was learning to listen to the world, to work with it, guided by the most ill-tempered teacher imaginable.

He felt a strange sensation, one he hadn't felt since

this whole nightmare began: a flicker of genuine excitement.

"A basin," he murmured to himself, already planning how he would explain it to Bak in the morning. He could already imagine the look on her face. It was going to be a long conversation.

5. The Quarry Quandary

The basin method had worked with a simplicity that bordered on the mystical. After a day of sitting under the sun, the water enclosed within the mud-brick wall had indeed found its perfect level. Marking the foundation stones and ensuring the subsequent courses were cut true had been a painstaking task, but it was one of precise measurement, not back-breaking guesswork. Bak had overseen it with a grim satisfaction, her initial skepticism towards Reni slowly being worn down by a grudging respect for results.

But a perfectly level foundation is useless without stones to put on it. And the stones, it turned out, were becoming a problem.

Reni stood at the edge of the plateau, watching the long, slow line of sledges crawling from the Tura quarries across the desert. Each sledge, laden with a monstrous block of white limestone, was a scene of orchestrated agony. Dozens of men strained on ropes, their chants a syncopated rhythm of pure effort. Others ran ahead, frantically pouring water from pots onto the sand, creating the slick path that allowed the sledge to move at all. But even with their new method, the pace was glacial. The sound that dominated wasn't the chanting, but the incessant, ear-grating screech of wood on damp sand.

"It sounds like a thousand cats being stepped on," a voice grumbled from a nearby pile of stone chippings. Khef had taken to disguising himself as inconspicuous debris when others were near. "Is that a necessary part of the process? The auditory torture?"

"It's the friction," Reni murmured, not moving his lips, a skill he was quickly mastering. "Even wet, it's a hard pull. We're going through water-bearers faster than we can recruit them. The quarry masters say they have blocks waiting, but we can't move them any faster."

"Friction," Khef mused, the stone chips shifting slightly. "You're still thinking of the sand as a surface to be overcome. A drag. A resistance."

"Isn't it?" Reni asked, watching another team of men stumble, the ropes going slack for a moment before they heaved again.

"Such a limited perspective," the spirit sighed. "You see a problem of pulling. I see a problem of flow. You are trying to drag a boulder through a substance that wants to behave like a liquid, but you're not letting it. You're just… wetting the top."

Reni frowned. "What else can we do? Drown the entire desert between here and Tura?"

"Don't be dramatic. It's tedious." The pile of chips was silent for a moment. "The sound is the key. The screech. It's the sound of countless grains being forced apart, shearing against one another and the wood. You need to reduce the shear. You need more water, but not on the surface. The moisture needs to penetrate. To create a true, low-friction slurry directly beneath the runner."

Reni tried to visualize it. "So… we dig a trench? Fill it with water and mud?"

"Crude, but getting warmer," Khef conceded. "But a trench would collapse. And require endless digging. No. The solution is already in your hand. The water pot."

Reni looked at the water-bearers, with their wide-mouthed ceramic pots. "I don't understand."

"The pot pours a stream. A temporary, surface-level dampening. What if the water was delivered... slower? More directly to the point of contact? What if it seeped, rather than flooded?"

Reni's eyes moved from the pots to the sledges themselves. He looked at the thick, curved wooden runners. An idea, half-formed and entirely stolen from Khef's prodding, began to take shape. "What if... we attached the pots to the sledges? Let them drip onto the runners constantly?"

Khef's pile of chips gave a slight, approving rustle. "The intellectual leap is staggering. Yes. A constant, slow drip. The water is drawn underneath the runner by capillary action, creating a permanent, thin layer of mud-slurry. The sledge essentially floats on a self-replenishing film of water and sand. The friction drops to almost nothing. The screeching stops. The pulling becomes... easier."

Easier. The word was like a drink of cool water. Reni

didn't wait. He walked down to the hauling track, Bak falling into step beside him, her expression questioning.

"We're changing the method," Reni said, his voice firm.

Bak simply nodded. She had learned that his "methods," while bizarre, tended to work. "What now? More water?"

"Different water," Reni corrected. He pointed to a sledge that had just been stopped for a rest. "I want a pot lashed to the front of this sledge, just above the runners. I want a small hole punched in the bottom, just enough for a slow, steady drip. I want the drip to land directly on the front of each runner."

The hauling crew looked at him as if he'd asked them to dance a jig. But Medju, Reni's ever-loyal guard, who had been assigned to the haulers for his strength, simply grunted, "Yes, Chief Architect." He found a pot, a length of rope, and a sharp stone to carefully chip a small hole. With a few efficient motions, he had the pot secured. Water began to patter down onto the sand in front of the left runner.

"Now, pull," Reni ordered.

The men took up the ropes, their bodies braced for the familiar, jarring resistance. They pulled.

The sledge lurched forward with a sudden, shocking ease. There was no screech. Instead, there was a soft, wet, shushing sound. The men, expecting a fight, stumbled forward, over-correcting. The sledge didn't just slide; it seemed to glide, the water from the pot seeping under the runner and turning the critical point of contact into a slick, flowing paste.

One of the haulers, an older man with a face like worn leather, looked down at the barely-visible trail of mud forming under the runner, then back at Reni. "It's... quiet," he said, his voice full of wonder.

A slow smile spread across Reni's face. "It is."

The order went down the line. Within an hour, every sledge had its own dripping water pot. The transformation was immediate and profound. The agonized screeching that had defined the quarry route was replaced by the soft, rhythmic shushing of wood on slurry and the relieved, almost cheerful chatter of the haulers. The pace of the stones arriving at the site doubled in a single afternoon.

Bak watched a fully laden sledge being pulled by a crew that seemed to be exerting half the effort they had that morning. She picked up a rope herself, feeling the difference. It was a smooth, steady pull, not a series of brutal, jarring heaves.

She walked back to Reni, who was trying very hard not to look insufferably pleased with himself.

"The stones are flowing now," she said, a statement of fact. "Like the river itself is carrying them."

Reni just nodded, looking out at the quiet, efficient line of sledges. He didn't need to claim divine inspiration this time. The result was its own testament. He glanced at the now-silent pile of stone chippings.

"Flow," he whispered to himself. It was a good word.

6. The Ramp Riddle

The pyramid was beginning to rise. The first ten courses of stone were in place, a broad, imposing square that was, thanks to Khef's water-level trick, perfectly true. But with height came a new and more daunting problem: the ramp.

Imhotep's original design had called for a single, massive, straight ramp rising against one face of the structure. It was a brute-force solution, and as the pyramid grew, the flaws were becoming monstrously apparent. The ramp was now a mountain in its own right, a vast earthenwork whose own construction was consuming more manpower and material than the pyramid itself. Its sides constantly threatened to slump, and its surface had to be widened daily to prevent sledges from sliding off the edge into the abyss. The groaning of the ramp under its own weight was a constant, low bass note beneath the work-site's symphony.

Reni stood with Bak at the ramp's base, looking up its dizzying incline. A sledge carrying a block for the eleventh course was stalled halfway up, its crew exhausted, the dripping water-pot doing little to ease the sheer gravitational defiance of the climb.

"This is unsustainable," Bak stated, her arms crossed. It wasn't a complaint, just a fatalistic observation, like noting the sun was hot. "We're building two monuments. One for the Pharaoh, and one to get the stones to the Pharaoh's monument. At this rate, the ramp will reach Memphis before the pyramid reaches the gods."

Reni didn't answer. He was waiting. Khef, in the form of a small, wind-blown pile of sand skittering around their feet, had been uncharacteristically quiet all morning.

"The straight ramp is an idiot's concept," the sand finally whispered, the grains swirling near Reni's ankle. "It fights gravity along the entire length. The higher you go, the more you fight. It's the architectural equivalent of head-butting a wall."

"What's the alternative?" Reni murmured, pretending to examine a crack in the ramp's side. "We can't levitate the stones."

"Must you always leap to the impossible?" Khef's whisper was dry. "Consider a snail. It does not attempt to scale a wall in a single, heroic leap. It takes a gentler path. A spiral path."

Reni blinked. He looked from the towering, precarious straight ramp to the rising, smooth-sided pyramid. "A spiral? Around the pyramid? But… the corners. The angles. It would be a geometry nightmare."

"For you, perhaps. For the stones, it is a gentle slope. A constant, manageable incline from base to peak. You trade a short, brutal climb for a long, easy walk. The ramp becomes a road, clinging to the structure itself. The higher you build the pyramid, the higher you build the ramp, simultaneously. One single, coiling effort, instead of two competing ones."

The idea was audacious. It was also terrifying. A spiraling ramp wrapping the growing pyramid like a coiled serpent. The logistics of curving the ramp at the corners, of ensuring it was supported by the pyramid's own courses… it was the kind of idea that would make Imhotep's eye twitch.

"They'll never agree to it," Reni said aloud, forgetting himself for a moment.

Bak turned from her contemplation of the stalled sledge. "Agree to what?"

Reni took a deep breath. There was no way to sugarcoat it. "We're tearing down the straight ramp."

Bak's head swiveled slowly towards him. Her expression was perfectly, utterly blank. "We are… what?"

"We're building a new one. A spiral. It will wind around the pyramid, from the ground to the top."

He waited for the explosion. For her to call him a fool, to list the thousand reasons it was insane.

She didn't. She just stared at him, her mind visibly working, her foreman's brain processing the concept. She looked at the straight ramp, a behemoth of packed earth and sand. Then she looked at the pyramid, a clean, geometric shape. She imagined a pathway coiling around it, a constant, gentle ascent.

"The straight ramp is killing us," she finally said, her voice low. "The men hate it. The engineers are terrified it will collapse and bury a hundred men. A spiral… it would use the pyramid for support. We wouldn't be fighting the structure; we'd be building with it." She fixed him with a piercing look. "The corners. How do we manage the turns without the ramp collapsing inward?"

Reni's mind raced, channeling Khef's logic. "We build the corners stronger. Use a tighter curve of stone and timber. The turning force will be distributed down the pyramid's face. It's… a more integrated system."

Bak was silent for a long moment, her gaze sweeping over the site, mentally dismantling the old and constructing the new. A slow, almost imperceptible nod. "It's either brilliant or it's the end of us." A grim smile touched her lips. "But at least it's not boring. The men will grumble. They hate changing a set routine."

"Tell them the straight ramp is an insult to the pyramid's perfect shape," Reni said, a sudden inspiration striking him. "Tell them we are building a path that honors the form, not one that assaults it."

Bak raised an eyebrow, a clear acknowledgment of the clever rhetoric. She turned towards the workforce and let out a sharp, carrying whistle.

"Listen up! Change of plan! We're giving the pyramid a staircase! Stop gawking and start dismantling the big ramp! We're building a new one that knows how to take a turn!"

As the groans and confused shouts rose into the air, Reni looked down at the swirling sand at his feet.

"A staircase," the sand whispered, its tone one of mild approval. "Not entirely inaccurate. For a snail, perhaps."

7. The Alignment Fiasco

The spiral ramp was a revelation. It was more than a practical solution; it was a thing of beauty. A gentle, rising roadway that embraced the pyramid, its curve a counterpoint to the structure's stark geometry. The workforce, after initial grumbling, had taken to it with a sort of possessive pride. It was their ramp, an innovation that set them apart from every other construction crew in history. The stones, once hauled up the grueling straight incline, now seemed to almost glide along the spiral path, the journey longer but far less brutal.

Reni, however, had little time to admire their handiwork. A new and more insidious problem was creeping in, one that couldn't be solved with water or a clever ramp. It was a problem of degrees, of almost imperceptible error.

He was in his makeshift office—a shaded area with a table covered in papyrus plans—when Bak found him. Her expression was grim.

"There's a lean," she said, without preamble.

Reni's stomach tightened. "A lean? Where?"

"South-east corner. It's slight. Maybe the width of

a finger over ten courses. But it's there. The level-men are arguing about it, but my eyes don't lie." She crossed her arms. "The foundation is true. The ramp is sound. But the stones themselves… the masons are the best we have, but they're human. A hair's breadth of error on one block, compounded over a thousand blocks…" She let the sentence hang.

This was the nightmare. A perfectly designed, brilliantly engineered pyramid that was, slowly and surely, turning into a leaning tower. The thought of Pharaoh Djoser's face when he saw his perfect mountain listing to one side was enough to make Reni feel faint.

He found Khef later that evening, the sand-spirit having taken the form of a small, weathered-looking rock nestled against the base of the pyramid.

"It's the human element," Reni whispered, leaning against the cool stone as if for support. "We can design perfect systems, but we can't execute them perfectly. The masons are tired. Their chisels dull. Their eyes strain in the sun. How do you command perfection from imperfect men?"

The rock was silent for a long moment. "You cannot command a river to flow uphill," Khef's voice finally emanated, a low rumble. "But you can dig a channel to guide it. You are trying to fight the error. To shout at the river. You must redirect it."

"Redirect a lean?" Reni asked, baffled.

"Not the lean. The masons." Khef's tone was that of a patient, if weary, tutor. "They are the river. Their collective effort is the current. Right now, the current is drifting. You cannot stop the current, but you can suggest a new direction. You need a story. A reason for them to correct the error themselves, without them even knowing they are doing it."

"A story," Reni repeated, skepticism warring with desperation.

"The stars," Khef said, as if it were the most obvious thing in the world. "Men look at the stars and see gods, patterns, omens. They fear them. Use that. The error is to the south-east. That is the domain of Sopdet, is it not? The star that brings the Nile's flood."

Sirius. The Dog Star. The herald of the inundation, both life-giver and potential destroyer.

"What about it?" Reni asked.

"Tell them the star-demons of the south-east are displeased. They see the pyramid as a rival, a man-made mountain challenging their celestial domain. They are pushing against it, trying to topple it. The slight lean is the first sign of their malice."

Reni stared at the rock, his mind reeling. It was absurd. It was superstitious nonsense.

"And how does that help us?"

"Because," Khef explained with infinite patience, "the only way to appease a star-demon is to show defiance. To prove the structure is too strong. The masons, in their work, must consciously—no, devoutly—ensure that every block on the south-eastern face is set just a fraction truer, with just a hair more care, to resist the demonic push. They will be correcting the error themselves, block by block, thinking they are engaged in a cosmic struggle. You are not commanding them to be more precise. You are giving their imprecision a villain to fight."

It was the most convoluted, ridiculous, and psychologically brilliant plan Reni had ever heard.

The next morning, he gathered the chief masons and foremen. He did not look like a panicked architect; he looked like a concerned priest.

"I have consulted the night sky," he began, his voice low and serious. "The pyramid draws the gaze of the heavens. Most gods look upon it with favor. But the spirits of the south-east, the jealous star-demons who guard the path of Sopdet, see it as an affront."

A few of the men shuffled uneasily. Bak watched Reni, her face unreadable.

"They cannot stop its rise," Reni continued, "but they press against it. You can see their influence—a subtle pressure on the south-eastern face. A test of our resolve." He let his gaze sweep over them. "We will not be swayed by celestial jealousy. From this day forward, every stone set on that face is an act of defiance. Check your levels twice. Ensure your joins are perfect. Let the demons see that the work of men, when dedicated to a god-king, is unshakeable."

He didn't mention the lean. He gave them a cause.

The change was not immediate, but it was profound. Over the following days, Reni watched the masons on the south-eastern side. They worked with a new, focused intensity. They conferred more, checked their plumb lines with a reverent care. It was no longer just a job; it was a sacred duty. The slight, creeping error didn't just stop; it began, ever so slowly, to reverse itself.

A week later, Bak reported to him. "The lean is gone," she said, her voice flat. "The south-east face is now the truest of all of them." She gave him a long, appraising look. "The star-demons, it seems, have been defeated."

Reni just nodded, a noncommittal sound in his throat.

As Bak walked away, a whisper drifted from a nearby pile of stone-dust. "You see? You do not fix the river. You simply give it a bank to follow."

Reni looked up at the pyramid, its silhouette sharp against the twilight sky. For the first time, he felt not like a fraud, but like a conductor, guiding a symphony of thousands, with a little help from a composer who understood the music of both stone and men.

8. Mutiny on the Mid-Level

The pyramid rose, a testament to unorthodox methods and the sheer, stubborn will of thousands. The spiral ramp coiled ever higher, a dusty brown serpent around a gleaming white mountain. But stone and sand were one thing; men were another. The initial awe at Reni's "miracles" had faded into the gritty reality of daily labor. A low, rumbling discontent began to brew, no longer about the work itself, but about the man directing it.

It came to a head on the mid-level, where the ramp made its fifth turn. The air was thinner, the sun hotter, and the view of the distant, green Nile valley a tantalizing reminder of a life far below.

Reni was checking the alignment of a new course when he felt the shift in the atmosphere. The usual rhythmic sounds of work—the chipping of chisels, the grunts of haulers, the shushing of sledges—had stilled. He looked up from his plumb line to see a circle of men, their faces hard and dusty, led by a brawny stone-hauler named Geb. Bak was standing slightly apart, her arms crossed, watching. She wasn't siding with them, but she wasn't stopping them either.

This was his problem to solve.

"The water was a good trick," Geb said, his voice a low growl that carried in the sudden quiet. "The ramp is clever. But we are not children, and you are not a god."

Reni slowly straightened up, his heart hammering against his ribs. "I have never claimed to be, Geb."

"You give us orders that make no sense. You change methods on a whim. You speak of star-demons and slippery sand." Geb took a step forward. "The men are saying you are touched by the gods. Others say you are touched by the sun. We don't know what you are, but we know you are not an architect."

Murmurs of agreement rippled through the crowd. They were not angry, not yet. They were uncertain. And uncertainty in a workforce of this size was more dangerous than any rage.

"You have us building a dream for a Pharaoh on the word of a scribe," another man called out. "We need to know there is a plan. A real one. Not just more… whispers."

Reni's mind raced. He could try to explain Khef. That would end with him being thrown from the pyramid. He could invoke the Pharaoh's name again, but that authority felt thin and brittle up here, so far from the palace. He had no divine vision to offer, no detailed blueprint. All he had were results, and that was no longer enough.

He looked at their faces, not as a faceless workforce, but as men: Geb, who had a new daughter he'd never seen; the young water-bearer with the limp; the old mason whose hands were a web of scars. They weren't challenging his authority out of malice. They were adrift in a sea of the unprecedented, and he was their captain, staring at a map only he could see—a map drawn by a sarcastic pile of sand.

He took a deep breath and did the one thing he had been avoiding since this began. He told them the truth. Or a version of it.

"You are right," Reni said, his voice quiet but carrying. "I am not Imhotep. I don't have all the answers. When the Pharaoh gave me this task, I had no idea how to build a pyramid. I still don't."

A confused silence fell. They had expected defiance, not confession.

"I look at these stones," he continued, gesturing to the massive blocks around them, "and I see problems. Problems no one has ever solved before. The ramp was collapsing, so we built a new one. The stones were too heavy to pull, so we made the sand slippery. The wall was starting to lean, so we fought back against the sky." He met Geb's gaze. "I don't have a grand plan. I have a series of problems. And when I face a problem I cannot solve, I do not look at the scrolls of the dead. I look at the world around me. I watch the water find its level. I listen to the sound the sand makes. I ask… what would work?"

He took a step toward them, his fear transforming into a desperate, earnest passion.

"Every one of you, in your trades, does the same. A mason feels a flaw in the stone with his hands. A hauler knows the exact moment to pour the water.

Bak knows the sound of a rope about to snap. You all solve problems every day. I am just doing the same, but on a larger scale. I am not a prophet. I am a… a noticer. And I am listening."

He paused, letting his words sink in. The men were still, their expressions shifting from defiance to contemplation.

"You want to know the plan?" Reni said, his voice growing stronger. "The plan is to build the Pharaoh his mountain, without getting buried by our own ramp, without breaking our backs on every stone, and without letting the sky push it over. The plan is to get this done, and for all of you to go home to your families when it is finished, with backs that are still straight and pride in what you have built. That is the only plan I have."

He looked around the circle, meeting their eyes one by one. "And I cannot do it without you. Your strength, your skill, and your patience with a scribe who is just trying to notice how the world works."

The silence stretched. Then, Geb grunted. He didn't smile, but the hostility had drained from his face. He turned, picked up his rope, and slung it over his shoulder. "The stone on sledge seven is shifting," he said, his tone back to business. "Needs to be reset before we haul it further."

It was not an apology. It was a reinstatement of the work. One by one, the other men turned away, returning to their tasks. The crisis was over.

Bak walked over to Reni as the sounds of work slowly resumed. "A 'noticer'," she repeated, her tone unreadable.

"It was the best I had," Reni admitted, his knees feeling weak.

She gave a single, sharp nod. "It was enough. For now." She moved off to bark an order at a group of haulers.

From a shadowed alcove between two massive stones, a trickle of sand whispered, so faint only Reni could hear it. "You appealed to their intelligence instead of their fear. A surprisingly sophisticated maneuver. Perhaps you are learning."

Reni watched the men work, a cohesive unit once more. He hadn't needed magic or threats. He had just needed to see them, and to let them see him. It was the most terrifying solution yet.

9. The Capstone Catastrophe

The pyramid was complete. Or nearly so. It was a breathtaking, impossible fact. A mountain of white Tura limestone, its sides smooth and gleaming, its geometry so perfect it seemed to have been grown, not built. The spiral ramp, its purpose served, was now a memory, its last traces being carefully dismantled by crews who worked with a kind of reverent awe for what they had accomplished. All that remained was the final piece: the pyramidion, the capstone.

This was no ordinary block. It was a single, massive, four-sided spike of electrum, a dazzling alloy of gold and silver, forged and polished to a mirror finish. It was meant to catch the first and last light of *Ra* each day, a blazing beacon announcing the Pharaoh's divinity for all eternity. It was also, by a significant margin, the single most challenging object to place.

It sat now on a reinforced sledge at the pyramid's base, a taunting, brilliant jewel. The problem was simple, absolute, and had brought all progress to a halt: there was no ramp left. The final course of stone was hundreds of feet in the air, accessible only by a sheer, smooth face. The capstone had to be lifted, not hauled.

Reni stood with Bak and the chief engineers, staring up at the summit. The wind up here was a constant, whining force.

"The leverage required..." one of the engineers, a man named Pesed, was muttering, scratching calculations onto a wax tablet. "Even with the largest counterweights, the pull of a thousand men... the ropes would snap. Or the capstone would slip. Or the men would pull each other off the edge. It is... it is not feasible."

"Feasible or not, it must be done," Bak said, her voice raspy from the altitude. "The Pharaoh arrives for the dedication ceremony in ten days. The capstone must be in place."

Reni said nothing. He was waiting. He had learned that in moments of true impossibility, a certain sandy presence often made itself known. He wasn't disappointed.

A small whirlwind of dust and chippings, easily mistaken for the constant wind, danced near his feet. "They are thinking of pulling," the familiar, dry voice whispered. "A vertical haul. How brutish. How utterly lacking in finesse."

Reni subtly shifted his position to block the wind-whisper from the others. "And what is the alternative? Pushing?" he murmured.

"Flying," Khef replied.

Reni choked, coughing to cover the sound. "Flying," he repeated, his voice a strained squeak.

"Must you always take things so literally?" Khef sighed, the whirlwind swirling with irritation. "Consider the seed of the sycamore. It does not strive to climb. It uses the air. It is carried. Your problem is not weight. It is imagination."

Pesed was now proposing a system of interlocking wooden cranes, a structure so vast and complex it would have taken a year to build. Bak was listening with a look of profound skepticism.

Reni's eyes were not on the engineers. They were on a group of children, the sons of the workers, playing in the dust at the edge of the site. They were flying a kite. A simple construct of reeds and woven papyrus, it danced and dove on the desert wind, a small, dark shape against the immense blue sky. A long cord tethered it to a laughing boy's hand.

It uses the air.

The idea was so absurd, so childish, that it felt like a physical blow. He looked from the dancing kite to the monstrous, gleaming capstone, then back again.

"He's lost his mind," Pesed whispered to Bak, noticing Reni's fixed, distant expression.

But Reni was already moving, striding over to the playing children. He knelt beside the boy with the kite. "Can I see that?" he asked, his voice gentle.

The boy, wide-eyed at being addressed by the Chief Architect, handed over the cord. Reni felt the pull, the lively, insistent tug of the wind on the simple craft. It was a powerful, constant force. A force that required no food, no wages, and never got tired.

He walked back to the stunned group of adults, the child's kite dancing at the end of its string behind him.

"We are not going to pull it," Reni announced, his voice clear and certain. "We are going to persuade the wind to carry it."

Bak stared at him, then at the kite, then at the four-ton electrum capstone. "You cannot be serious."

"We will build a cradle for the capstone," Reni said, the plan forming in his mind as he spoke, guided by an invisible, sandy prompter. "A harness, not of rope, but of the strongest woven cables. And we will build kites. Not one. Dozens. The largest ever made. We will attach them to the cradle."

Pesed let out a sound somewhere between a laugh and a sob. "Kites? To lift the pyramidion? The weight... the instability... it is the most ludicrous—"

"It is the only idea that doesn't involve certain death and a shattered capstone at the bottom of this pyramid," Reni interrupted, his gaze steady. "The wind is a force. We have been using forces all along. Why not this one?"

The following days were a frenzy of what looked like utter madness. The finest sail-makers from the Nile's shipyards were summoned and set to work creating enormous, reinforced kites from the strongest linen. A special harness was woven around the capstone. The workforce, now possessing a near-fanatical faith in Reni's brand of insanity, threw themselves into the project with a curious energy. After building a pyramid, what was a few giant kites?

The day of the attempt dawned clear and windy. Perfect. The capstone, in its web-like harness, sat on a specially greased stone slide that angled up the final face of the pyramid. Dozens of the massive kites, each the size of a small boat, were laid out on the ground, their lines gathered in the hands of the strongest and most trusted haulers.

A hush fell over the entire site. Thousands of faces looked up. Pharaoh Djoser himself was reportedly watching from a shaded pavilion miles away.

"Release the kites!" Reni shouted.

The haulers ran, and the kites, catching the wind, billowed and then shot into the sky. They strained at their lines, a flock of gigantic, frantic birds. The lines tightened, connecting to the harness. The woven cables grew taut, humming with a deep, resonant thrum.

For a long, heart-stopping moment, nothing happened. The capstone remained stubbornly on its slide. Pesed buried his face in his hands.

Then, with a groaning shudder, the great electrum point shifted. It lifted, just a finger's breadth, from the stone.

A collective gasp swept the plateau.

"Ease the lines! Let the wind take it!" Bak bellowed, her voice cracking with tension.

The haulers, working in a coordinated dance, let the lines slip through their gloved hands, controlling the ascent. The kites pulled, the wind sang in the cables, and the capstone began to rise. It was slow, majestic, and utterly silent save for the hum of the lines and the roar of the wind. It didn't look like it was being hauled. It looked like it was being offered up.

It floated, impossibly, up the final face of the pyramid, a gleaming offering to the sky. As it neared the summit, teams of masons waiting at the top guided it with long poles, slotting it perfectly into the prepared base.

The moment it clicked into place, a perfect, seamless fit, a silence more profound than any before fell upon the world. Then, a roar erupted from thousands of throats, a sound of pure, unadulterated triumph.

Reni stood, his legs trembling, watching the capstone gleam in the sun. It was done.

From a patch of sun-warmed stone at his feet, a quiet whisper emerged. "You see? You did not fight the weight. You invited the air to a negotiation." A pause. "It was… almost elegant."

Reni didn't answer. He just looked at the finished pyramid, a perfect, geometric mountain against the sky, and for the first time, he felt not like an impostor, but like he had earned the seal he carried. He had noticed, he had listened, and he had built the impossible. With a little help from a friend who understood the wind.

10. The Return of the Prodigy

A week after the capstone was set, a palpable, festive energy hummed across the Giza plateau. The pyramid was complete. The workforce, still camped around the site, was engaged in the final tasks: clearing debris, polishing the lowest courses of limestone, and preparing for the grand dedication ceremony. There was a sense of collective disbelief. They had done it. They had built the impossible. And Reni, the scribe-turned-architect, was at the center of it all, moving through the crowds with a quiet authority that no longer felt borrowed.

He was reviewing the final inventory of tools with Bak when a ripple of unease passed through the workers. The casual chatter died down, replaced by hushed murmurs. Reni looked up, following the collective gaze towards the causeway that led from the Nile valley.

A man was walking towards the site. He was lean, weathered, and dressed in the simple, dusty linen of a traveler. But his posture was ramrod straight, and his gaze swept over the finished pyramid with the piercing, analytical intensity of a master craftsman.

It was Imhotep.

He looked older. His face was tanned and lined from months in the desert sun, and his beard, once neatly trimmed, was now a wild, grey-flecked thicket. But his eyes, the eyes that had calculated stresses and strains until they broke, were clear and sharp. He stopped a hundred paces from the pyramid's base, his head tilted back, taking in the sheer, impossible scale of it.

Reni's blood ran cold. The seal of the Chief Architect, which had come to feel like a part of him, suddenly felt like a stolen object burning against his hip.

Bak let out a low whistle. "Well," she said, her tone dry. "The prodigy returns. And he doesn't look like he's found his sanity. He looks like he's found… answers."

Imhotep's eyes continued their methodical journey, tracing the flawless lines, the perfect angles, the breathtaking apex where the electrum capstone blazed in the morning light. His expression was unreadable, a mask of pure observation. He saw the clean-swept ground where the straight ramp had been, the lack of any massive, external lifting structures. His gaze lingered on the polished stones, the perfect joints. There was no collapse. No chaos. Only majestic, silent perfection.

Finally, his eyes landed on Reni. He began to walk forward, his steps slow and deliberate. The sea of workers parted before him, a silence of profound awkwardness falling over them all.

He stopped a few feet from Reni. He did not greet him. He did not acknowledge Bak. His eyes were fixed on the pyramid behind them.

"It is standing," Imhotep said, his voice hoarse from disuse, but still carrying that familiar, precise clip.

"It is," Reni replied, his own voice thankfully steady.

"The capstone is in place."

"It is."

Imhotep finally turned his gaze to Reni. It was not angry. It was deeply, profoundly curious. "How?"

It was the question Reni had been dreading for months. The one he had no real answer for.

"We… adapted," Reni said, choosing his words with the care of a man crossing a rickety bridge. "The initial designs presented… challenges."

"Challenges," Imhotep repeated, the word tasting foreign in his mouth. "The straight ramp was a failure. I see you have no ramp at all. How did you lift the stones to the upper courses?"

Reni's mind raced. He could not say 'a spiral ramp.' The evidence was gone, dismantled. "We developed… an internal system," he said, which was technically true, if wildly incomplete.

Imhotep's eyes narrowed. "An internal system." He looked back at the pyramid, his mind visibly working, trying to fit this new, shapeless data into his rigid understanding of physics and logistics. It didn't fit. "And the capstone," he pressed, his voice gaining a slight edge. "Four tons of electrum. Hauled to that height without a ramp. How?"

Reni felt a trickle of sweat run down his back. He saw Bak watching him, her face neutral. He could not say 'kites.' "We utilized… countervailing forces," he said, the phrase sounding as hollow as he felt. "We worked with the environment."

Imhotep took a step closer. The scent of desert dust and bitter herbs clung to him. "Worked with the environment," he echoed, his voice dropping to a near whisper. "Reni. I walked away from this site because the problems were insurmountable. The mathematics did not support the ambition. I have spent months in the desert, studying the wind-sculpted stones, the way sand settles, the fundamental principles of the world, trying to find a different path. And I return to find… this." He gestured to the pyramid, a note of something like anguish in his voice. "A monument that, by all rights, should not exist. And you, a scribe, stand before me speaking of 'countervailing forces' and 'internal systems'. You will explain this to me."

This was the moment Reni had feared. The confrontation. The exposure. He was saved, for the moment, by the arrival of a royal messenger, his linens crisp and clean, a stark contrast to the dusty workers.

"Acting Chief Architect Reni!" the messenger announced, his voice ringing in the silence. "Pharaoh Djoser, may he live forever, will arrive tomorrow for the final inspection and dedication! All must be prepared!"

The title 'Acting Chief Architect' hung in the air between Reni and Imhotep like a slap. Imhotep's face, for the first time, showed a clear emotion: a flash of raw, unadulterated fury, quickly suppressed.

"Acting," Imhotep said, the word a poison dart.

The messenger, noticing Imhotep for the first time, did a double-take. "Master Imhotep! You have returned! The court is abuzz with the news! Your timing is fortuitous. The Pharaoh will be most eager to hear of your... travels, and to receive your professional assessment of the completed project."

The messenger bowed and scurried away, leaving a silence even more charged than before.

Imhotep looked from the retreating messenger back to Reni. The fury was gone, replaced by a cold, calculating calm. He had been gone. The project had been completed in his absence, by a junior scribe using methods he could not comprehend. His legacy, his life's work, was being handed to an upstart who spoke in riddles.

“It seems,” Imhotep said, his voice dangerously soft, “that we will both have an audience with the Pharaoh tomorrow. I look forward to your… explanation then. I am sure it will be… enlightening.”

He gave the pyramid one last, long look, a mixture of awe and bitter resentment in his eyes, then turned and walked away, heading towards the administrative quarters he had once abandoned.

Bak let out a long, slow breath. “Well. That could have gone worse.”

“How?” Reni asked, his shoulders slumping. “How could it possibly have gone worse?”

“He could have started screaming about dark magic right here in front of everyone,” Bak said pragmatically. “Instead, he’s going to do it in front of the Pharaoh. It’s more civilized.”

Reni groaned, pressing the heels of his hands against his eyes. He was back in the nightmare. The pyramid was built, but the most dangerous obstacle had just walked back into his life.

Later, in the privacy of his own simple quarters, Reni slumped onto a stool. A small, familiar pile of sand was stirring in the corner.

"The original architect has returned," Khef observed, his tone implying he'd been watching the entire drama with academic interest. "He seems… displeased that his catastrophic failure has been transformed into a triumphant success."

"He knows I didn't do this," Reni whispered, his head in his hands. "He knows it's impossible. He's going to tell the Pharaoh I used sorcery or… or made a deal with a desert demon."

"The latter is technically correct," Khef noted. "Though 'consultant' is the preferred term."

"This isn't funny, Khef! He's going to have me executed! All he has to do is ask me to explain the principles behind the kite-lift or the spiral ramp in detail, and I'm finished!"

"Then you must not let him," Khef said, as if it were the simplest thing in the world.

"And how do I do that?"

"You must speak a language he cannot refute. The language of results." The sand-figure shifted, taking on a more defined form. "This Imhotep is a man of logic. He believes only in what can be calculated and proven. Your entire project is an affront to that belief. You cannot win a debate with him on his terms. So, you must change the terms."

"To what?"

"To the only thing that truly matters to your Pharaoh," Khef replied. "The monument itself. Do not try to explain the 'how'. Emphasize the 'what'. You did not build his pyramid. You delivered his vision. You took an impossible dream and made it stone. Imhotep saw only problems. You saw… possibilities."

Reni looked up, a flicker of understanding cutting through his panic. "He'll say it's trickery."

"And you will ask him to point to the flaw," Khef's voice was a firm whisper. "Challenge him to find a single crack, a single misalignment, a single engineering failure in the entire structure. He will not be able to. His logic will be defeated by the evidence. A thing that cannot exist, does."

It was a gamble. A huge one. It relied entirely on the pyramid's perfection being its own defense.

The next day, the royal court descended upon the plateau in a cloud of dust, perfume, and dazzling regalia. Pharaoh Djoser was radiant, carried on a litter, his eyes fixed on his mountain with a look of pure, childlike joy.

"Reni!" he boomed, as he was helped from the litter. "My visionary! You have done it! You have built my stairway to heaven!" He clasped Reni's shoulders, beaming.

It was then that he noticed Imhotep, standing to the side, waiting with a stiff, formal bow. "Imhotep! You are returned! Come, look! Look at what has been achieved in your absence! Is it not magnificent?"

Imhotep stepped forward, his face a carefully composed mask. "It is a staggering achievement, Your Divine Majesty. Truly… unprecedented." He paused, letting the word hang. "So much so, that I confess myself… baffled. The methods used are… unfamiliar to the architectural sciences."

The Pharaoh's smile didn't falter. "Methods? Who cares about methods! Look at it! It's perfect!"

"Perfection is often an illusion, Divine One," Imhotep said, his voice smooth as oiled stone. "I am concerned that unconventional, perhaps even... unstable... techniques may have been employed. Techniques that could compromise the eternity of your rest."

The courtiers murmured. Djoser's smile tightened just a fraction. "What are you saying, Imhotep?"

"I am saying, Your Majesty, that this young man," Imhotep said, gesturing to Reni without looking at him, "has accomplished what I, with a lifetime of study, deemed impossible. I merely wish to understand how. For the security of your eternal monument. Surely, the Chief Architect can explain the principles that ensure this mountain will not one day crumble?"

All eyes turned to Reni. The moment had come. He could see the trap, laid out with impeccable precision. He felt the weight of the court's gaze, the Pharaoh's growing doubt, and Imhotep's cold, triumphant expectation.

He took a deep breath, remembering Khef's advice.

"The Master Architect is correct to be vigilant," Reni began, his voice clear and carrying. He did not look at Imhotep. He looked only at the Pharaoh. "The eternity of your house is all that matters. And so, I would like to propose a test."

A ripple of surprise went through the crowd. Imhotep's eyes narrowed.

"A test?" Djoser asked, intrigued.

"Yes, Your Majesty," Reni said. "Let Master Imhotep himself be the judge. Let him inspect the pyramid. Let him use all his skill, all his knowledge, all his measuring tools. Let him examine the foundation, the joints, the alignment of the capstone. Let him search for any flaw, any instability, any sign of the 'unconventional techniques' he fears. If he finds a single, verifiable weakness… then I will concede that my methods were flawed."

He finally turned to Imhotep, meeting his gaze squarely. "The pyramid is the proof, Master Imhotep.

Not my words. The stone does not lie. Will you accept this challenge? Will you put your doubts to the test?"

The court fell utterly silent. It was a masterstroke. Reni had not defended his methods. He had put the entire burden of proof on his accuser, using the very monument Imhotep coveted as the witness for the defense.

Imhotep was cornered. He could not refuse without looking like a petty jealous man. He looked at the perfect, gleaming pyramid, a structure he had already, with his own expert eyes, judged to be flawless. To 'inspect' it was to confirm its perfection, and in doing so, confirm Reni's triumph.

His jaw tightened. A muscle twitched in his cheek. He gave a short, sharp bow to the Pharaoh.

"As you wish, Divine One," he said, his voice strained. "I will… inspect the monument."

But everyone could see the truth in his eyes. He had already lost. The pyramid itself had defeated him.

11. Sand in the Royal Court

The inspection was a formality, a silent, day-long procession of defeat. Imhotep, trailed by a handful of his own loyal engineers and watched by the entire court, subjected the pyramid to the most rigorous examination imaginable. They used polished bronze mirrors to reflect sunlight into the deepest joints, searching for gaps. They hung plumb lines from the soaring faces, finding only perfect verticals. They measured the base diagonals, confirming the perfect square. They even, at Imhotep's increasingly desperate command, had workers tap every stone on the lowest course with bronze mallets, listening for the hollow sound of a poorly set block. They heard only the solid, resonant thud of perfection.

With every test, Imhotep's shoulders slumped further. His face, once a mask of superior intellect, became a drawn parchment of frustration and awe. He was being systematically dismantled not by a man, but by a mountain. A mountain that defied his every expectation.

Finally, as the sun began to set, casting the pyramid's long shadow across the desert, he was compelled to stand before Pharaoh Djoser and deliver his verdict. The court assembled once more, the air thick with anticipation.

"Well?" Djoser demanded, his patience worn thin by a day of what he saw as pointless prodding. "Will my eternal home stand, or has this boy built me a tomb of playing cards?"

Imhotep stood before him, looking older than he had upon his return. He clasped his hands tightly in front of him to keep them from trembling.

"The structure…" he began, his voice hoarse. He cleared his throat. "The structure is sound, Your Divine Majesty. The workmanship is… impeccable. The alignment is true. There are no flaws that I can discern."

A wave of relieved murmuring swept through the courtiers. Reni felt a tension he had been carrying for months finally uncoil in his chest.

"Then what is all this nonsense about unstable techniques?" Djoser pressed, his eyes narrowing.

Imhotep's gaze flickered to Reni, a flash of pure, undiluted bitterness. "The methods remain… unorthodox. Unproven in the annals of architecture. The long-term stability of such… innovations… cannot be guaranteed."

It was a weak, pedantic retreat, and everyone heard it.

Reni knew this was his moment. He stepped forward, not with aggression, but with a calm finality.

"Your Majesty," he said, his voice quiet but clear. "Master Imhotep is a scholar of what has been done. I… was tasked with what could be done. He looks at a stone and sees its weight, its resistance. I was forced to look at that same stone and see its potential for flight. He sees the desert as an obstacle. I learned to see it as a partner." He gestured to the flawless pyramid behind him. "The result is not a rejection of his knowledge, but an extension of it. We both sought to serve you. I simply took a different path."

He had given Imhotep an olive branch, wrapped in undeniable victory. He had not gloated. He had reframed the entire conflict not as a battle between right and wrong, but between tradition and innovation, with the Pharaoh's glorious mountain as the prize.

Pharaoh Djoser beamed. This was a language he understood. Drama. Vision. Triumph.

"A different path!" he echoed, clapping his hands together. "Yes! A path that led to my mountain! Imhotep, your counsel has always been valued. But you yourself said it was impossible. Reni did not. That is the only difference that matters." He turned his radiant smile upon Reni. "The title 'Acting' is hereby removed. You are the Chief Architect. This monument will be known for all eternity as the Layer of Reni!"

It was a colossal honor, one that stole the breath from Reni's lungs. He saw Imhotep physically flinch, as if struck.

The matter was settled. The court erupted in applause and congratulations. Imhotep stood frozen for a moment, a statue of obsolescence in the shifting sand of progress. Then, without another word, he turned and walked away, not towards the palace, but back into the vast, empty desert from whence he came. This time, no one expected him to return.

As the celebrations swirled around him, Reni caught a whisper on the wind, a voice only he could hear, tinged with something almost like respect.

"You appealed to the vanity of a king and the pride of a builder. You did not defeat your enemy with facts. You made him irrelevant. You are learning the most subtle art of all… politics."

Reni didn't reply. He just watched the solitary figure of Imhotep disappear into the twilight, the price of his own success suddenly feeling very heavy indeed.

12. A Monument to Mayhem

The dedication ceremony was a blur of incense, chanting, and roaring crowds. Pharaoh Djoser, in a state of ecstatic delight, officially named the structure the "Layer of Reni," a name Reni knew would be forgotten by history, replaced by something grander and less personal. It didn't matter. As he stood watching the festivities, the gleaming pyramid felt less like his achievement and more like a fact of the landscape, as if it had always been there and he had merely been the one to notice it first.

In the quiet of the evening, with the workmen's campfires glittering below like a fallen constellation, Reni found himself alone at the pyramid's base. The sense of accomplishment was profound, but it was tinged with a peculiar loneliness. The frantic, daily crisis was over.

A familiar, gritty voice broke the silence. "They are already telling stories," Khef said. The sand-spirit had resumed his preferred form—a small, compact figure seated on a stone, his dark eye-holes reflecting the starlight. "They say you were taught by Thoth himself. That you whispered to the stones and they obeyed."

Reni smiled faintly. "They wouldn't believe the truth."

"The truth is often duller than fiction," Khef replied. "And far less flattering to my contributions." There was no real sting in the words, only a dry, familiar warmth. "The binding is complete. The task is done. My nap awaits."

This was the moment Reni had been quietly dreading. "So you're leaving."

"The noise is abating. The constant, grating vibration of problem-solving has ceased. It is... peaceful." Khef stood, his sandy form crunching softly. "You no longer need a consultant. You have become what you pretended to be. A rather capable 'noticer'."

It was the highest praise Reni could imagine receiving from him. "Thank you, Khef. For everything. I would have been measuring sand without you."

"Do not sentimentalize it. It was a contractual obligation." The spirit took a step and began to dissolve, his form softening back into loose, unremarkable sand. "Try not to awaken any other ancient beings with your frantic prayers. We are notoriously grumpy."

And with that, the sand settled, still and ordinary. He was gone.

Reni felt a sharp pang of loss. Then, as he turned to go, he saw it. Sitting precisely where the sand-figure had been was a tiny, perfect pyramid, no taller than his thumb, meticulously formed from packed, dark sand. It was a flawless, geometric mountain.

He picked it up carefully. It held its shape, a solid, silent gift. A monument to their mayhem.

Smiling, he placed the tiny pyramid in the palm of his hand and walked back towards the lights and the life below, ready for whatever came next.